Win Your Arguments
Without Being Labeled a

AnswerGirls

First edition: copyright © 2015 by Panoply Press

Print Edition:
ISBN-13: 978-1-882877-46-1
ISBN-10: 1-8882877-46-2

Kindle Edition:
ISBN-13: 978-1-882877-47-0
ISBN-10: 1-8882877-47-8

All rights reserved. No part of this book may be reproduced without permission from the publisher, except by a reviewer who may quote brief passages in a review; nor may any part of this book be reproduced, stored in a retrieval system, used on the internet or copied by mechanical photocopying, recording, or other means without permission of the publisher.

Printed in USA

Book Design: Northwest Publishers Consortium
Cover and text photographs: istockphoto.com

Published by:
PANOPLY PRESS
PO Box 1885
Lake Oswego, OR 97035
panoplypress@gmail.com

TABLE OF CONTENTS

Who are the AnswerGirls? 5

Introduction 7

Chapter 1 Not All Arguments Are Created Equal 13

Chapter 2 Time Out for An Attitude Check 23

Chapter 3 Don't Bet on A Dead Horse 35

Chapter 4 Pick Your Time & Place 47

Chapter 5 The Opening Gambit 59

Chapter 6 First One Who Ramps It Up Loses 73

Chapter 7 Don't Like Your Opponent's Arguments? Rewrite! 81

Chapter 8 The Body Language of Arguments 93

Chapter 9 Beef Up Your Arguments 105

Chapter 10 Get Ready to Nail That Agreement 115

Chapter 11 The Win! 127

Chapter 12 Negotiating for Fun And Profit 137

Index 140

"Like a thunderstorm on
a muggy summer day,
a rousing good argument
can really clear the air,
though the air smells
a whole lot sweeter
when I win."

Anne Lindsay

WHO ARE THE ANSWERGIRLS?

The AnswerGirls, authors of this series, are a team of women, spunky, talented and funny. Coming from many different careers, professions, ages and experiences, these Kindle-packin' mamas have a take on life that's straight to the point on the outside, feisty and flip inside.

Together, they have a solution for many of the problems plaguing modern women. From dating and marriage to parenthood, family life and work, the AnswerGirls cover it all. Excellent advice like you've never heard it before.

Speaking woman-to-woman, they teach you how to bite back and love it! Learn what it takes to get ahead in a man's world while enjoying life to the fullest. AnswerGirls' books support the sisterhood with the goal of putting all women on the path to a better life.

Would it surprise you to learn that most self help books for women are written by men? Sad but true.

This series is different; our books are written by women!

One AnswerGirl writes each book, but as you read you'll encounter advice from several other women, each identified only by her label. The secrets and advice these women share are not for the opposite gender. Although there's nothing to prevent men from buying our books, they're written for your eyes only.

And, since men generally purchase books written by men, especially when it comes to understanding women, we think our secrets are safe.

Now get ready to win your arguments!

INTRO

If you could win all of your arguments—every single one of them, including squabbles with your lover, disputes with your parents, tiffs with your kids, disagreements with your boss, or spats with your grumpy neighbor—what amazing power you'd have! You'd be well on your way to ruling the world!

How about winning all quarrels with your co-workers, fallings-out between friends, and differences of opinion between you and the I.R.S.?

Yeah, well, we all need our pipe-dreams. The odds of that happening every single time are slim to none. But what if you could win most of those arguments? Wouldn't that definitely be a step in the right direction?

Certainly that's a marketable skill, one that most people, including world leaders, would envy.

Let me tell you, it's not an impossible goal to achieve.

To many of us the word, "argument" is like a line drawn in the sand. You're here—the other person is there—let the battle begin!

But let me note for the record that this mindset doesn't help you win arguments. And it often ends in a victory no one can savor, especially when tremendous hurt has been inflicted by one or both sides.

In situations like that, can anyone really call herself a "winner"? Do you really want to stand on the battlefield, having vanquished your opponent, only to realize that the tactics you've used have left you standing alone in your victory, with no one left to watch your victory dance, let alone help you celebrate?

That's the fastest way to being labeled, "Supreme Bitch." If that sounds appealing to you, go ahead and give it a try. But I can tell you right now that there's a much better way to win, one that's extremely satisfying and lets you get most or all of what you wanted in the first place.

Introduction

" I'm so angry with a certain guy who's acting like a real ass—and if you think "ass" is too strong a word to say in print, you have not met this man. Right now the notion of me being known as Supreme Bitch sounds awfully good.

I've put up with too much from this man and I'm so tired of it. He accuses me of something (more like ten things) every day, usually containing no element of truth. I find that I'm forced to defend myself day in and day out. It really drags me down.

So let me set the record straight, I want to be a Supreme Bitch. I want to put him in his place and keep him there. I need to do that for my children's sake and for my own. So I'm going to be reading this book with great motivation, and I want to end up a Winner. But please don't tell me I can't be a bitch. "

Well, if you want to be known as a bitch, I've just told you how to get that title. But I'm here to say you can do a lot better than that. I guarantee the novelty of the title wears off after a while, and it can be difficult to dump a label like that. I assure you, that there is a far more satisfying victory waiting for you, and for all women.

By the end of this book, you'll have a formula for winning arguments in such a way that your opponent may not even realize he's lost. You won't have to pillage and burn the entire village just to get your message across. And it's likely he won't be back for re-runs. I know that by the time you finish reading this book, you'll be wondering why holding the title of Revenge Queen was once so important.

Let somebody else be... Revenge Queen!

I speak from decades of experience. After starting life as a quiet, shy, but intelligent child, I realized in my teens that I was often on the losing end of battles, a victim and not a happy one!

So I set out to change that. It took years and years of concentrated effort, because I had no road map to follow. I just knew where I wanted to end up.

Long-term stints as a wife, mother, employee, employer, business owner and even as a multi-term elected official all have given me knowledge and have helped me hone my arguing skills.

Being an analytical person, I studied my methods, determined to figure out the system behind a successful argument, if indeed there was one. And I'm happy to report that there is.

What you'll find in this book is a blueprint for women who want to master successful arguing. It's also a formula for negotiation. The more you practice this formula the better your skills will become, and the easier and more satisfying your interpersonal relationships will be as a result.

In this book, I'll walk you through the steps to a win, starting with a review of the types of arguments you'll encounter and a check on your attitude.

Later we'll study which arguments you'll want to engage in, plus learn techniques for dealing with each. You'll even find help in tidying up the playing field and achieving the satisfaction of a job well done.

Arguments will naturally find you, but if you start using these rules, you'll get plenty of good practice and learn how to win.

1

Not All Arguments Are Created Equal

If you've ever been hijacked by an argument during an otherwise hot date, or tried without success to convince a Seahawks fan to root for the Patriots, you've discovered the truth that all arguments are not created equal.

Let's take a brief look at the whole gamut of arguments, good, bad and otherwise.

Fuzzy, Warm, Good Sport Arguments

There are fuzzy, warm arguments—the kind you'd never expect to win and wouldn't know what to do if you did. But hey! Who's going to pass up a chance to try to get your Republican brother-in-law to vote for a Democrat? Or speculate on the future of mankind living on Planet X?

If you're the kind of person who loves the thrill of an argument at a coffee house or family gathering, you probably love to jump into the fray with both feet and debate the night away. Yahoo!

These can sound ferocious, but usually aren't. Although your Great Aunt Hester could develop chest pains over what seems like an out-and-out family feud, these arguments don't usually cause lasting injury. At the end of the evening everyone hugs everyone and your brother-in-law goes home, still determined to vote Republican. No one expected a different outcome, although a few of the younger family members remember this as the night they came to believe in the colonization of Planet X, wherever it may be.

This is arguing for the love of it. It's great entertainment, with no winners, no losers.

Earnestly Intellectual Arguments

The world is full of intriguing mysteries that have become the perennial fodder for intellectual argument, like these:

- Are what appear to be man-made structures on the moon evidence of a super race of visiting aliens who are watching us from afar?

Chapter 1: Not All Arguments Are Created Equal

- Did Shakespeare write some, all, or none of his plays? Did philosopher Francis Bacon sneak a secret code into those "Shakespearian" plays he, himself, may have written?
- Was Beethoven poisoned by his doctor, or did he die from alcoholism?

These arguments are the stuff of cable TV and esoteric club meetings, as experts and would-be experts on both sides of an issue pound their points. Are they winnable arguments or speculation? Or maybe speculation strengthened by a hint of science?

For most of us, these earnestly intellectual arguments are pure entertainment. Feathers get ruffled, but except for rare and unusual circumstances, no one gets hurt. For the historians or scientists who've made these theories their life work, such arguments may someday be winnable, but only as history and science reveal further secrets. Until then, we look on and speculate. No wins here, at least for now.

Arguments Based on Crazy "Facts"

Some arguments are so bizarre that you almost choke when you hear them. They're based on spurious facts, such as, "the moon is made of blue cheese." That's just one that comes to mind, but others are much more subtle. Recognize these for what they're worth—utterly and hopelessly not winnable.

Arguments Based on Sincere Opinions

In the teachers' lounge at the local elementary school, an argument lasted several days: Would education be improved if the children were given a shorter lunch period and an earlier end-of-day release, or not?

No one could doubt the sincerity of the debaters. Some teachers argued that very few children go home for lunch, so a full hour is far longer than needed to eat and play. Others voiced their opinion that young children in today's society are allowed so little free play time after school that this noon-hour opportunity should not be overlooked. Still others expressed concern that an earlier after-school release time would cause difficulty for working parents.

There you have it: all valid points and all sincere opinions. These arguments are winnable, and well worth discussing.

While some of the arguers might be wedded (or welded) to their opinions and some might have hidden private agendas ("I'd give my entire lunch hour to get home earlier!"), these arguments are reasonable discussions. They can get heated, but the flames are not deliberately set. That doesn't mean, however, that in this type of argument no one will get hurt. Opinions can be sincere, but unintentionally inconsiderate.

Sometimes a person's sincerity is questionable. An example of this could be parents discussing whether or not to send the children to summer camp. Or it could be a couple debating whether to buy a house.

I use the words "could be" because, depending upon the circumstances, either of these arguments could be conducted with less than sincere motives. For example, is one parent arguing against camp, with the malicious intention of preventing the other from being free to accept a summer job?

As for the new house, is one individual's obstinate stand based on retaliation for a previous affair? If the opinions aren't sincere, these arguments belong in another category, Arguments Intended to Hurt or Maim.

"Tired & Cranky" Arguments

After staying up late the night before, watching taped reruns of NFL games, your husband comes home from work (where he was denied a promotion), and he lets loose.

"There's dog hair in every corner that's been there forever (or so he says), your spaghetti Bolognese tastes like crap (or so he claims) and why can't you quit that loser of a job and stay home like a good wife?"

If you are able to sidestep that argument, he'll go at you for overspending on the grocery budget. If you were his mother, you'd send him to bed without dinner, but alas, you're on call to deal with this argumentative spouse.

If this is your problem, don't despair because help is on the way. You can learn to deal with tired and cranky arguments effectively, by postponing or stopping them, as I'll teach you in Chapter 3. However, it's situations like these that can lead blindly into the following category.

Perennial Arguments, No Longer, If Ever, Valid.

Any argument has the potential for immortality. Suspect a Perennial Argument whenever you hear the same charge leveled at you time and again, and you know it's false.

These repeat offenders are easy on the one who starts them, and annoying for the receiver. If, at some moment in history, the argument was based on a somewhat valid fact, that moment hasn't been seen since before the Vietnam War. Yet the arguer keeps insisting, year after year, that you hate Southerners, love dogs more than cats, or think motorcycle boots are "cute for weddings."

Perennial Arguments ... are like really Bad Habits!

Perennial arguments are nothing but bad habits. And, like any bad habit, the "period of unlearning" takes time and persistence. But again, like any bad habit, it can be broken.

Arguments Intended to Hurt or Maim

Now we move far from the realm of annoying and into the really serious stuff. Plenty of everyday arguments are like torpedoes—they seek a target and aim to hurt or destroy. Even arguments that to an outsider may seem benign can be hurtful and cruel, depending upon the intent of the instigator. These arguments are a form of mental abuse, keep that in mind.

> The courts take mental abuse very seriously, because it can often be even more harmful than physical abuse. Repeated arguments that are intended to hurt or maim can cause trauma,

Chapter 1: Not All Arguments Are Created Equal

> depression and a host of other psychological problems for women who are subjected to this behavior.
>
> Quite often these arguments are a form of domestic abuse, when it's a partner or spouse who's involved, but the mental abuse could also be perpetrated by a parent, boss, relative or domineering "friend" (if you'd even want to call her that.)
>
> I'm glad to see you mention that not all arguments are the warm, fuzzy type. Women should understand that they don't have to put up with verbal abuse. If you're afraid to take legal action, knowing how to avert these malicious arguments will help to deflect verbal attacks.

Arguments intended to hurt usually have emotional undertones. You might think that these would only be launched by those closest to you, but that isn't necessarily true. Sometimes the arguer's reasoning might even be quite obscure.

Public figures often face arguments that are intended to hurt from unknown individuals, acting with unknown motives.

However, many hurtful arguments do come from a friend or loved one, based on perceived injustice. These are the truly nasty ones because emotions can run deep. You can learn how to win them, but unless the underlying psychological scars are healed, they may be re-launched again and again. By using more effective techniques for winning, it's possible to neutralize them.

So that's the range of arguments you're likely to encounter. You may be the instigator yourself, in which case you'll want to be sure you've studied the closing moves. As you've seen in this quick overview, your chances of winning varies considerably, depending on the type of argument, so later on we'll take a closer look at how to handle each type.

2

Time Out for An Attitude Check

Oh, how I wish colleges offered degree courses in Arguing! Don't you agree that would be one of the more useful survival tools for life, and a great benefit to civilization as a whole?

But wait! Some colleges do offer them—only they're not called "Arguing 101"—they sound far more professorial when they're listed in the catalog as "Negotiation 101." Not a bit of difference, really. However, that points to an interesting problem: the word "arguing" has apparently been blacklisted.

Why is "argument" a negative term in English, and especially in American English? So negative, in fact, that "negotiation" is deemed to be a more positive synonym.

Although the verb, "to argue" can also mean to examine and discuss both sides of an issue, "argue" is mostly considered to be destructive and something to be avoided, while "negotiate" and "debate" are wonderful, positive words that mean substantially the same thing.

This leads Americans to believe that arguing is a bad activity, and negotiating or debating are perfectly good activities. This, I believe, is the reason we as a culture have difficulty handling an argument. We don't see it as a positive activity, so we dredge up negative words and feelings to describe it.

Let's do an attitude check, before we start winning arguments.

Call An End to War!

To successfully learn to appreciate arguing as an art form, we must first remove the stigma that all arguments are evil. So, instead, let's think of them as negotiation, which is not only acceptable, but praised. Arguers are to be scorned, negotiators are given the key to the city.

I'm saying, if you want to win arguments you need to stop artificially inflating them to the status of a nuclear blast. Feel free to change the word argument in this book to negotiation if that helps you with this concept.

Chapter 2: Time Out for An Attitude Check

And while I'm on my soapbox, there's more! Let's swap out other confrontational words that are often used in reference to arguments, words like battling and battlefield, fight, combat, and any other word pertaining to war.

Gearing up for An Argument

When you prepare for war, you put on your camouflage gear, flak helmet, or chain mail armor. You pick up your weapon and turn on your most aggressive self.

But if you're getting ready for a soccer match or hockey game, you suit up differently. Forget the ammunition and quit pushing the cannon to the battlements. The persona you adopt should be competitive, not combative.

Rethink this!

25

And what a difference that makes! It's the difference between sportsmanship and pure aggression.

If you adopt the belligerent language of war and fighting when referring to an argument, this shapes the tone of the discussion. If instead, you treat that discussion as a sporting event, it stays competitive and winning is far more satisfying.

Here's the difference: when we treat an argument as sport, we now have a playing field and sports gear, we even have a victory. But it's not a "vanquishing victory," it's an honest, healthy win. Avoiding antagonistic and belligerent words and actions takes the sting out of arguments.

So how do we manage to change our mindset? Through conscious effort and practice. It doesn't happen overnight. If you change your attitude, you'll see a change for the better in your opponent's arguing style as well.

This is particularly useful when your opponent is aggressive. By making sure you switch your inner language to that of competitive sports, the mindset follows easily, and the tone of the argument shifts.

Chapter 2: Time Out for An Attitude Check

Let Your Brain Practice Arguing

Changing bad habits—or developing good habits—requires ongoing practice. It's quite amazing what the brain can accomplish if you get out of its way and let it do what it does best.

Back in the 1980s, Dr. Maxwell Maltz wrote books on the subject of psycho-cybernetics, a technique for allowing the brain to teach the body to master certain feats. As an example, people were tested on their ability to throw a basketball into the hoop.

Subjects took turns shooting hoops, and the results were tallied, counting successful shots for each participant. Then the volunteers were divided into three groups: A, B and C.

Group A did nothing after the test for the following two weeks. They were specifically instructed not to play basketball, and to just go about their daily routines.

Members of Group B practiced shooting hoops for two hours each day.

The members of Group C, after being tested, did not touch a basketball for the entire two weeks. Instead, each night before they went to sleep they would visualize the process of shooting a ball successfully into the hoop.

"The mind is a powerful tool if we learn to make use of it."

They were told to see and feel this clearly in their mind: "feeling" the weight of the ball, "concentrating" on lining up the shot, "throwing" with as much precision as they could, and "hearing" the sound of the ball dropping through the basket. And of course, "hearing" the cheers of the crowd!

At the end of two weeks each participant was tested again, against his or her previous score. It was no surprise that the members of Group A didn't improve their skills during that period, and again, it came as no surprise, that the Group B players' skills did improve.

The real shocker was that Group C members, who didn't touch a basketball, but who instead visualized the process of shooting, also improved dramatically, just like the group that had physically practiced. This test was tried with other sports and, in each case, the power of the mind improved a sports skill without physical practice.

Yeah, But Arguing's Not Really A Sport

So, you might ask, what's that doing in a book about Arguments—which are not exactly a physical skill? Well, arguing is a learned skill, just like shooting baskets. The more practice you get, the more adept you become.

I often hear people say, "If only I'd joined the debate team in school." I know I've heard myself say that in the distant past. And sure, that would have been fabulous practice. But don't beat yourself up over it. There are other ways to become better at arguing, without the agony of a faceoff with a silver-tongued opponent.

Not on the team? No problem!

So if you missed the boat for the Debate Team, realize that through the magic of psycho-cybernetics, you can visualize arguments and their resolutions, and become quite adept at it.

For each of the techniques I describe in this book, simply visualize your winning moves again and again.

Watch your attitude (remember this is sport, not the battle of the Alamo), then visualize, visualize, visualize.

" This is very powerful stuff! The mind is amazing in its capabilities. When I was in college, our class did an experiment with psycho-cybernetics

Chapter 2: Time Out for An Attitude Check

while studying for a biology test. One group studied, the second didn't, and the third read the text once, before sleeping, and then visualized passing the test.

We got the same results! The visualization helped immensely, and the third group did almost as well as the group that had studied far into the night. The group that hadn't studied did exactly as expected.

Personally, I'm glad to be reminded of this technique. I was too scared to join the Debate Team, and have always thought I would have been amazing at negotiations if I'd done that.

I'm happy to hear that I can compensate for it by practicing in this way, and that I don't have to find argumentative people to practice with. This is definitely doable!

I do think that deliberately engaging the mind turns on the switch to some powerful brain activity. In fact, I think we'd all do well to use this technique more often in everyday life.

Tah! Dah! The Winning Mindset

I have one more secret to share here, and this one will seem far too easy to be effective. Here it is:

Know that you will win.

That's my secret and it's a powerful one. Your attitude must be utterly positive. If you're not convinced that you'll win, why are you wasting your time arguing? No one else will believe your argument if you don't.

Picture a coach in the locker room before the game: "Players, they'll be looking for every last opportunity to sock it to you, but you're better that that—wa-ay better. You know you've got what it takes. You know you're gonna bring that trophy home with you!"

Okay…since we're now treating arguments as a sport, this is the very least we can do for our players! Yay! Go Team Go! Be your own very best supporter.

> "Winning easily gets to be a habit. Sadly, so can losing."
>
> Joan Jeffers

Chapter 2: Time Out for An Attitude Check

So What Does It Take?

Is it true that simply by knowing that you'll win, using non-combative language, and practicing in your sleep you can win your argument every single time?

Nope. All of those are essential, but we're just getting started. If the art of winning arguments were that easy, you wouldn't need this book.

To return to our basketball analogy, even if you mastered the art of free throws, whether by shooting hoops or psycho-cybernetics, you still wouldn't know the rules and techniques for winning. And of course the sport of arguments is exactly the same.

What you still need is a framework for that argument, essentially the Ground Rules. And that's what you'll learn in the following chapters.

So now that you're suited up and you've got your attitude aligned just right, you're ready to learn the steps involved in winning arguments. As you read this book, you'll be building up your technique, layer by layer until you finally know what it takes to win.

The next layer calls for great discernment, deciding how to separate the wheat from the chaff when it comes to arguments. Although you may feel compelled to voice your opinion whenever an argument presents itself, you must learn to discriminate.

Never place a bet if the team hasn't a snowball's chance on a hot tin roof of winning. And the same applies to arguments.

> "It takes exactly as much time and effort to develop a good habit as it does to adopt a bad one. So choose your habits wisely."
>
> Joan Jeffers

3

Don't Bet on A Dead Horse

If you go to the racetrack and suggest to your friend (or maybe your enemy!) that he bet on the horse that just died on the way to the starting gate, you'd be astounded if he followed your suggestion.

Yet do you realize how many arguments are attempted that have—just like the dead horse—a zero chance of survival, let alone a win? I can tell you: an almost infinite number!

But you're smarter than that; you'd never bet on a dead horse, right?

That's where you need to be discerning. You need to evaluate an argument right at the starting gate. Never begin or enter into arguments that can't be won, or shouldn't be argued. Not only is this a waste of time, it's demoralizing to put yourself into a losing position automatically.

> "If you want to spend your time arguing with a thunderstorm, have at it. But wouldn't it be smarter just to step under cover? I'm all for smart!"
>
> Mary Hetherington

We've briefly talked about a few of these arguments, but let's elaborate. These disputes, which can't possibly be won, are guaranteed to blindside you when you least expect them.

I'll explain later what to do if an unwinnable argument hits you out of the blue, but first let's identify the various types of unwinnables.

Provocative and False Accusations

One example of a provocative accusation that can't be won goes something like this:

"You're so argumentative, that's all you ever do."

Think of it—if you argue back, you're proving that you're prone to arguments! Winnable? No!

Or this one:

"You're so stupid, you don't know when to shut up."

Don't tell me you'd even consider arguing this point!

Crazy-Loonies

Some arguments are based on a verifiable lie of outrageous proportion, such as:

"The government is deceiving us when they say the earth is round."

Or: "Congress voted last year to take away a woman's right to vote."

Back off immediately!

And don't touch this one either:

"Pregnancy is a condition that affects 9 out of 10 teenage girls these days."

If the "facts" are as crazy as you think they are, argue these at your peril. My advice would be to run from them, and in this chapter, I'll show you how to do that like a winner too.

> "His so-called facts were about as solid as melted ice cream."
>
> Danielle M. Forester

Arguments That Aren't Yours

There are some arguments that you simply aren't meant to enter into. A good example is an argument that follows a traffic accident.

You're standing in the middle of the intersection, after having had your car hit from behind as you tried to make a left-hand turn. The driver who hit you is arguing, "You're not supposed to turn left there, you didn't signal correctly and it's all your fault."

Don't go there—this isn't your argument. This one belongs to your insurance company or the lawyers. When an argument should be debated by professionals, let the professionals take over. Simply exchange information and let them deal with the other driver. The less said the better.

Chapter 3: Don't Bet on A Dead Horse

You may be surprised to know that many people are unable to walk away from an argument they shouldn't be getting into. Please use better sense.

> Have you noticed how addictive arguments are? They're like eating peanuts—you get started and you just can't put the bowl down.
>
> I always want to save the world—only the world doesn't always want to be saved. I can tell you that if I saw you standing in the middle of the intersection after your accident, I'd be out of my car, arguing your case for you! Not sure if I'd be winning. Maybe I should have been a lawyer.
>
> I have definitely got to learn how to be more restrained in my arguments. But it's in my blood! Family entertainment in my house wasn't TV, it was arguing. Every night at dinner it would take less than five minutes for an argument to start.

> And we'd go at it hot and heavy, banging on the table to make a point, sometimes long after dessert was over.
>
> Since I left home, I haven't found anyone who loves to argue like my family. I suppose that could be the reason why I'm not married! 99

Another example of an argument that isn't yours would be one that starts while you're over at your sister's house when the neighbor knocks on the door to complain about your sister's nuisance tree that's dropping leaves on his patio.

It's fine to share tips privately with your sis, but this situation is hers to deal with. Don't jump in and argue.

Arguments That Are Smart to Avoid

Some arguments could possibly be won, but ask yourself, would it be smart to do so?

A good example of this is what you might encounter on the front line dealing with customers at work. Let's say you're behind the counter at a fast food restaurant, and an irate customer says, "You put cream in my coffee and I wanted it black," when

Chapter 3: Don't Bet on A Dead Horse

he actually had said no such thing. Now you could argue back, "You didn't say that at all. You're stuck with it, buddy."

But what a useless argument! It's your word against his, and over a one dollar cup of coffee? And of course what your supervisor might think of your PR skills if you did that, could be enough ammunition to get you fired! Deal with it like an adult, smile and pour another cup.

> "I was a little loose with my opinions, but she was definitely loose with her facts."
>
> Bronwyn S. Banks

Your Underlying Assumption

With any argument you choose to engage in, you must have one underlying assumption and you must never, ever waver from it. That assumption is that there is at least one solution to this argument, and it will be one that you will be satisfied with.

If you work with this assumption in mind, the argument formula outlined in this book will be much easier to follow, because this assumption sets a goal for you.

If you're not fully committed to winning this argument, always ask yourself, "Why am I arguing?" Stop the argument immediately if this is the case. Later in this chapter you'll learn how to do just that.

Visualize Your Assumption

Here's how I like to draw my mental picture of an assumption. I am holding two pieces of very thick cord and I must find a way to join them, so that I can make a longer cord. How am I going to do that?

I could take the ends and tie them together in a knot. But knots work their way loose and are bulky, so that's not a perfect join.

I might be able to splice them—taking the strands apart and weaving them together—but still that's not an invisible join and could come unwoven.

What I really need is a way to fuse the ends together, so that magically and invisibly, the two cords become one. And that's exactly what I'm going to do in my argument. With every step, I will picture the fusion of the ends.

It's truly amazing how your brain will follow this instruction, and work to reach that result if you just keep the assumption in your mind.

Stop an Argument on a Dime

There is one nifty technique that you need to have up your sleeve, and that's the ability to stop an argument instantly, for whatever reason. The solution sounds simple, but that's the beauty of it. The arguer will be expecting much, much more of a rebuttal from you, and I'm reasonably certain it will leave him or her speechless, giving you plenty of time to exit, stage left.

Let's take a sample argument and see how it works. Your husband comes home from work to find you nursing a sick baby, cooking pork chops and trying to get a proposal finished for work, while the rest of the children are climbing the walls. And he says: "You spend way too much time on the computer and not nearly enough time keeping an eye on the kids. They're turning into little monsters and they need to develop a sense of responsibility about putting away their toys."

Unless you can successfully counter this argument at the present moment, don't even try. Stop this man right now. You can always discuss the finer points of the issue later.

So if you're a smart woman, not a masochist, and if you want this argument to stop in its tracks, your response is either, "You're right," or (somewhat less effective), "Good point!"

What–you used my technique on ME??

I love it! I even had it used on me last week. I had an impassioned argument all planned, points to be made, conclusions to be reached, against a very stubborn opponent. When I came up for air after my opening salvo in round one, expecting to go a full ten rounds, he said, "Sure."

Well—if I'm allowed to mix sports metaphors and, hey, it's my book—that took the wind out of my sails pretty darn quick!

If you're in the habit of picking up the bat and stepping up to the plate (I am shameless about mixing metaphors!) when an argument is tossed at you, and you try this technique, the astonishment on your opponent's face will be well worth the smile you're going to be forced to hide!

Take Control of Your Arguments

Honestly, who can continue to argue if it sounds like you agree? This is not losing; this is putting a stop to any argument whenever you need to. This technique puts you in the driver's seat at a time when you need to be there. I don't take credit for developing it myself. I picked up this tip from author and speaker, Mary Robinson Reynolds, and it's certainly valuable.

If you feel a response is needed, but you can't quite bring yourself to say, "You're right," try something similar like, "Point well taken!" or, "You've got a point!" or, "Amazing!" These words are especially useful when you are being asked to debate something that's utterly crazy-loony.

We'll take another look at this technique later, in Chapter 7, and we'll expand on it in other situations as well, where you might want to continue the argument, but only on your terms. For now, the important thing to remember is that you have control over which arguments you decide to engage in. The choice is yours whether to proceed or to stop an argument in its tracks.

And just knowing that control is in your hands is a pretty powerful feeling.

4

Pick Your Time & Place

Winning an argument is absolutely about power and control. And that means, wherever possible, controlling the time and location to your advantage.

Just as duels of yore were scheduled at sunrise in the meadow, or 3 pm at the OK Corral, successful arguments should have a specified time and place. And to win, you need to choose a time and place to your liking.

Of course, that's not always possible. If your time of choice is fixed and inflexible, for instance, each Sunday at 9 am, lots of luck scheduling your disputes that rigorously!

But that doesn't mean you have no control whatsoever. You just need to expend some effort in drawing up the ground rules. This chapter will show you how to do that.

Worst Times to Argue

Your chances of winning are increased if you're prepared for the argument, and feel well physically and mentally. Chances are decreased if you are either ill-prepared or not in top condition.

Here is a list of times to avoid:

- when you're tired,
- when you're sick,
- when you're under stress,
- when you're busy or pre-occupied,
- when you're not feeling confident,
- when you haven't had time to prepare,
- when you're with others,
- when you're feeling very angry,
- in the morning if you're a night owl,
- at night, if you're a morning person.

Chapter 4: Pick Your Time & Place

> Girl, I hear you speaking my name!!! I dread it when my husband picks a time to argue when most of those bad factors converge and the kids pick up on it. I find myself at the worst possible time, with a houseful of Tired & Cranky arguers, and I somehow have to have enough wits about me to respond. How is this possible?
>
> I have to let you know, this is not easy!! I don't want to stop the argument completely, but need a quick hack to make it disappear, at least for now, until my sanity is restored (which I hope will happen before the kids leave the nest and that's no time soon.)
>
> When I have a houseful of children—his, mine, ours, wonderful as they all are—I am definitely not in top form for an argument a great part of the time.
>
> So I can't begin to tell you how much I need help here!

I hear you, loud and clear. Sounds like you have a junior Greek Chorus that picks up the theme from your husband and drowns you out when you're least able to handle it.

Read on, and I'll teach you how to postpone the argument at least until the kids are in bed and your wits are assembled.

Put It Off Until You're Ready

With your busy schedule, it may be impossible to pick the perfect time. But perfection isn't the goal here. Just know that if you aren't up to par, postpone it. You must make every attempt to argue at your convenience.

Any argument is better postponed, giving you prep time.

But wait, you say! My boss, who's trying to pick an argument that my work ethic leaves much to be desired, won't sit back and be gracious when I say, "Nope, sorry. Not arguing right now, I wanna reschedule." Well, of course, you're not going to be saying that—or would you? Only if you'd love an excuse to be fired.

But I'm going to give you the power to postpone your arguments to a more satisfactory time, without your opponent going ballistic. In fact, your opponent may not even realize you're buying yourself some serious prep time.

Standing in Your Power

The popular expression, "to stand in your power," describes a state of readiness, self-confidence and inner strength. To win an argument, you need to be standing in your power, and that comes only with preparation.

Stand up tall, take a deep breath and recognize that you do have the inner strength to handle this situation, if you give yourself permission to do so. Call on your self-confidence resources and give yourself that permission—before you say a word.

I like to picture my body with a strong inner core. My spine is holding me straight, I'm looking the world in the eye and I have the confidence to hold my own in any argument.

Only when you're standing in your power are you ready to begin.

> **"You have to have confidence in your ability, and then be tough enough to follow through."**
>
> Rosalynn Carter

Don't Answer, Acknowledge

Let's go back to the argument we talked about, where your boss is complaining about your sadly missing work ethic. Your boss throws it at you suddenly, 4:45 on Friday when all you can think of is meeting your friends at the pub and celebrating the start of the weekend.

The very worst thing you can possibly do (other than throw something and burst into tears) is to attempt to answer her allegations. Don't even think of it! Instead, you need to find a way to acknowledge her concerns, and postpone the discussion until you are in peak form, with a ready-made plan for your rebuttal. And that is certainly not going to be tonight!

Here's how to do it. The acknowledgment (said very calmly) sounds something like this:

"That sounds like a matter we really do need to discuss. I'd like to give it some thought. Would Monday right after lunch break be a convenient time to talk about it?"

You're not rushing to protest, you're acknowledging her concern and you're scheduling a response. It was all done in a way that works well for you. But what'll you say when Monday comes? That's for another chapter. Right now, we're talking about ways to acknowledge an issue and buy time to prepare to address it.

Consider the acknowledgment a validation of your boss's concerns. That often satisfies an arguer for the time being. While she or he may be itching for a rousing debate, validation that these concerns are of importance is not a bad response, and the delay is usually accepted.

Admittedly, there are some moments of heavy emotion, where both parties feel the need for the argument to take place right now. And some arguments have a time factor built in, like a debate about whether the children should be allowed to stay up right now to watch a movie.

However, an argument postponed is more likely to be an argument won.

More Ways to Acknowledge

The words of an acknowledgment can vary. Here are other magic phrases to consider:

- "Oh! I hear what you're saying and I can see it's definitely a concern for you. This is something we should address, don't you think? And the sooner we schedule a time to do it the better."
- "You've got a point there. Let's walk on our lunch hour and talk."
- "Hmm…I'll have to think about that. Give me a couple of hours and let's discuss it."

Sometimes you can't buy days or even hours to prepare. When that happens don't give up hope, stall for a couple of minutes by customizing the following statement to fit the setting, just to give you time to evaluate both the accusation and your quick strategy:

- "Oh! I hear what you're saying and I can see it's definitely a concern for you.

> This is something we should address, don't you think? Shall we get a cup of coffee and sit down and talk about it?

Recognize that when another person makes a statement that seems to be the lead-in for an argument, he already has a whole quiver full of poison-tipped arrows, ready to aim straight at you. When you give yourself the time to plan your strategic replies, your inner strength will protect you.

Location, Location, Location!

We've discussed the timing of an argument, now let's think about the place for it. The best location for an argument is a spot where you feel strongest, whether it's in your office, the living room or the city park. When you schedule your argument, choose the place that suits you best.

One place to avoid, if possible, is your opponent's home turf—his office, for instance, conference room, home or gym. And avoid a place that's unfamiliar to you. Psychologically, an unfamiliar spot requires the body to expend energy acclimating itself to its surroundings. Your whole focus and energy should be on the argument, not on how unusual the color scheme is, or how uncomfortable the chairs are.

Standing is powerful, so consider a location where you can stand, or to give the appearance of standing, like leaning on a tall counter or against a wall. Avoid, like poison, a situation where you are seated on a soft cushy sofa, while your opponent paces or sits in a hard chair facing you. In fact, stay away from soft sofas and armchairs entirely.

If you find you're forced to accept an argument in an office other than yours, suggest that you both sit on the visitors' chairs. If he's seated behind the desk, stand, or at the very least, pull a visitor's chair off to the side so he's not facing you over the desk top. Desks are automatically powerful, so try to stay away from any discussion in your opponent's office.

Your office on the other hand, would be a place of power for you, especially if you have a ridiculously soft, low sofa that robs your opponent of his sense of control.

Pick a Color Scheme

No kidding! Hire an interior decorator to schedule an argument? Well, no, but not a bad idea!

Each of us feels our best in a particular color or color range, and this is the color scheme for your

Chapter 4: Pick Your Time & Place

argument. You probably are aware of colors you like and colors you look good in. Some people come alive wearing red, and for them, red would be a good choice for an argument—a red room and a red sweater.

Black is always powerful, and many women find the contrast of black and white extra empowering. If pink makes you feel like a little girl, don't argue in a pink room wearing a pink sweater. Contrast and clarity are important. A dreamy pastel patterned blouse will never be as authoritative as a plain shirt and dark suit jacket or dark sweater.

Of course, how ridiculous to think if an argument crops up and you're wearing pink fuzzy jammies, you have to say, "Excuse me. Hold that thought while I change!" But if you have the time to make a choice, choose wisely.

> "From the sidewalk to the top step of the front porch, Lila and Uncle Jay would choreograph their arguments like a Broadway play."
>
> Carin Faulkner

So now you've bought yourself some time, and chosen a perfect location. You're wearing your favorite high-impact color and feeling wonderfully empowered. Now it's time to step into the argument and find your winning path.

The next step is the opening gambit, giving you control of the argument right from the start.

5

The Opening Gambit

The stage is set. Let the argument begin.

For those readers who don't play the game of chess, a gambit is a strategic starting move that often involves some risk, losing a pawn, for instance, with an eye on the ultimate win. What I like to call the "gambit" in an argument is a little different—pure strategy, of course, and some risk, but with the goal of winning.

In our opening gambit we will give away nothing, *nada*, not a single pawn or secret strategy. So here's how it works.

If this is an argument that has been foisted on you, it may go something like this:

"Why can't you follow the rules like all of the other club members? You don't see them playing such obnoxious golf!"

Ooh…got it! The instigator's message is flashing like a huge neon sign in the desert at midnight. No matter what you happen to think about this fellow club member, or her accusation, do not state your position. Don't lash out and tell her what you think.

Instead, first you acknowledge, and then you buy yourself some time.

You've Everything to Gain by Buying Time

So here's what you might say to accomplish that:

"I can see this is something that's been bothering you, and I agree with you that we should talk about it. How about we meet for coffee on the patio at 11?"

Validation of her concerns, followed by scheduling an argument that buys you time.

Most opponents will readily agree to a suggestion like that. After all, you just said that you agree their concern merits discussion. Presumably by 11 am, you will have assembled your thoughts, read the rest of this book and are standing in your power.

When you meet at 11, let your opponent begin. If a bet were possible here, I'd say she's calmer and

Chapter 5: The Opening Gambit

not coming at you so aggressively, although some instigators use that time to fortify their case with even more accusations.

Whether she comes at you now with:

> "Your flagrant disregard for club rules is troubling to those of us who come here for a relaxing game of golf,"
>
> or: "You can't go around here acting like you're Queen Bitch,"
>
> or: "I have to tell you, your stupid, inconsiderate behavior has got to stop,"

or all of the above, you will need to respond. How you do it will determine the course of the entire argument.

For the sake of discussion here, I'm going to assume that you don't agree with the assessment. Because, if you did agree, you'd end the argument quickly with a simple, "You're right, " and maybe even make a new friend who thinks you're so perceptive because you agree with her!

No matter how she phrases it, don't give away your position. This is chess, right—you don't tell her what plans you have for capturing her king.

Take a Tip from a Toddler—Ask Questions

You can protect your game plan by asking questions. Your strategy is to hear all of hers, and she will gladly lay it out for you, because your opponent is eager to get it off her chest and be proven a winner.

As you ask your questions, phrase them so they validate *part* of her argument. When I say, "validate," I don't mean roll over and agree with her that, yes, you're indeed an obnoxious golfer who doesn't know the rules.

Validation is simply an agreement that her concerns are important to her, something I think you'd readily acknowledge, having just heard her hot-tempered accusation. So here's what you say:

"I can see this has been troubling you. [validation] Would you tell me specifically what your greatest concern is? [question]"

Validate + Question... then ditto!

Don't use words that echo her accusation. For example, don't ask, "What is it about my behavior you think is so obnoxious?" By repeating her accusations, you've just acknowledged them! You've just opened yourself up to even more accusations of a similar or greater intensity.

If you mention "obnoxious behavior," now she's got to go one better. And you've just let her take your queen.

Why Not Defend Myself?

You'll have plenty of time to defend yourself later, but the purpose of the opening gambit is to allow you to hear all of her arguments without revealing any of your positions.

Think about what you've just been handed, when she answers your opening question. You know exactly what's annoying your accuser, and you know precisely how strongly she feels about it.

In order to advance her argument, she'll have to supply even more information to bolster her point, and with each question you ask, your opponent will provide more, right up to the level of her irritation.

I'm sure most of you would agree that sounds like a pretty smart tactic. The benefit to you is that you have managed to get a copy of your opponent's entire strategic plan, without giving her a single hint as to what the arguments in your defense might be.

It's Okay to Be A Sponge

Absorb all the information she's willing to send your way, because soon her supply of arguments will be exhausted, while you have yet to reveal your first strategic move.

If you reveal your position too early, you've lost the argument and provided your opponent with the opportunity to think of new rebuttal points. But if you wait until she's used up all her points and is reduced to repeating her accusations until even she's sick of hearing them, you can win your points far more easily.

That, in a nutshell, is our strategy.

Ask More Questions!

Take a tip from psychiatrists, who are known to speak only in questions. There are reasons for this technique: first, it forces the patient to express in words his or her own picture of the problem, and second, it keeps the therapist's own thoughts from clouding the issue. The same reasons are valid here.

By asking clarifying questions, you are not evading the issue. On the contrary, you're acknowledging it with interest. (Something that's flattering to your opponent.) However, it's important to phrase your questions correctly, because you never want to provide your opponent with an opportunity to regroup and use your questions against you.

Here are some suggestions for our "obnoxious golfer" argument:

- "Do you have any additional concerns you feel we should discuss?"

This is an interesting question, because the word "concerns," as opposed to "allegations," "accusations" or "beefs," is an acknowledgment of the seriousness of the instigator's claims, yet it's a fairly neutral word that points to the person with the concerns, rather than to the accused. It also expresses your willingness to listen.

- "I see...could you give me a few details on exactly what you're concerned about?"

Again, validation with the word "concern" and the question indicates your interest.

- "Got it! And are there changes you'd specifically like to see?"

Leave any mention of your own behavior out of it and just ask in general terms.

> **"I always cheer up immensely if an attack is particularly wounding because I think, well, if they attack one personally, it means they have not a single political argument left."**
>
> Margaret Thatcher

Don't Let Your Opponent Bolster Her Defense

An interesting study was conducted in 2012 at the University of Colorado, by four researchers led by Philip M. Fernbach. Although it primarily dealt with political extremism, the results are applicable to the art of argument as well.

The researchers discovered that if proponents of an extreme political view were asked to give their reasons for holding such a view, the act of listing reasons actually reinforced their belief in this view.

But if the researchers asked them to explain how their view *could be put into practice*, the very explanation was apt to cause them to rethink their position. And the likelihood of a change of attitude was higher than if they'd been asked to list reasons.

The instigator of an argument holds strong views. So if you ask her the reason for her views, based on this research, you can expect that her views will likely be reinforced.

During the course of some arguments, it can be difficult to differentiate between the two types of questions—reasons vs. explanation. So don't take a chance on either if you're not sure.

But in every case, do avoid asking your opponent why she holds such views.

> It's so natural for us to ask others with opposing views why they hold those views. So this research is very interesting, as it confirms the opposite: that we should avoid doing that, probably at all times.
>
> I know I've seen many instances where this has happened to me—like during a discussion with another doctor about the preferred medical treatment.
>
> And if I find myself disagreeing, every time I've asked the other person for reasons why he or she believes that would be the best course to follow, I can see his or her defenses rising.

Chapter 5: The Opening Gambit

> And all of a sudden, a discussion can turn into a full-blown argument.
>
> It's very interesting to discover that by changing the question and asking the other doctor instead to explain how to use the treatment, no defense is necessary. I must remember that.

Back to the Work Ethic Argument…

Here are some suggestions for the argument we introduced in the last chapter—the boss's argument about your lack of work ethic on the job:

- "Uh huh! I do see your concerns. Could you perhaps elaborate about what concerns you most?"
- "I'm glad we're taking the time to discuss your concerns. Is there anything else?"

Have you noticed that the ambiguous word "concern" plays a major role in these responses, usually along with the word "you" or "your."

First of all, it's truly flattering for someone to have his or her concerns acknowledged, even if you have no intention of actually addressing them at this point.

And second, it's putting the focus on the instigator, who really wanted the focus to be on you and your shortcomings!

However, I would bet that the boss is getting so much satisfaction from relating all your misdeeds (and finding a ready audience) that she has not even realized that your comments all turn the focus back to her and to her "concerns."

This is why you can feel positive about your handling of the argument so far. You're not capitulating at all, you're listening, and that's essential for winning any argument.

What if You're the Instigator?

So far, we've just discussed an argument from the point of view of the accused. If you are the one who started the argument, I hope you will read this entire book to see what techniques could be used against you and how you can counter them.

For example, if the opponent asks questions and turns the focus to you, be canny about how much information you give out during the gambit. You can, and should, even ask questions yourself, with the hope of prodding the accused to argue her case

Chapter 5: The Opening Gambit

from the start. If she instantly goes on the defense, that's excellent for you, the instigator.

Her rebuttal will give you plenty of information about her position, so that you can take her comments and shape the argument your way. You'll find out how to do this later in the book.

Don't give information.

So to recap what I call the Gambit portion of an argument, you are, first, acknowledging your opponent's position and beliefs, and, second, asking questions to discover his or her strategy.

You are gathering information, but not yet sharing any. Remember this technique is true for whichever side you find yourself on in an argument, whether you are the instigator or accuser.

It's sometimes difficult, when we have been sucked into an argument, to avoid lashing out at our accuser. Don't do it! Keep in mind that you will have your day in court, and it will come at a time after your accuser has shown you his or her entire strategic plan and has finally run out of steam.

And you haven't even ruffled your hair. It really can't get better than that!

6

First One Who Ramps It Up Loses

So you think this formula's all too mild mannered to ever win an argument? Wondering when you'll get to rant and rage? Think again. Bitches don't win arguments, canny women do.

I can guarantee that the first person to ramp it up will soon be declared the loser.

If you remember back to the various types of arguments, there were some pretty raucous ones that no one expected to win, like trying to convince a dyed-in-the-wool Republican to vote for a Democratic candidate. Not likely to happen, but the argument is loud and fun.

The arguments we're talking about winning are of the more serious genres, not only everyday business or interpersonal disputes, but the type intended to hurt the opponent.

There's no fun in these, just the challenge of winning and sometimes the stakes are high.

Don't Rise to the Bait

The tone of your argument should be firm and quiet, no louder than your normal speaking voice. Even if the accusations are hurtful, raising your voice in anger won't emphasize your point.

Think of it this way: your opponent, especially one who is out to make you suffer, will feel he's achieved a measure of success with every decibel you raise your voice. If he can incite anger and make you lose your cool, he knows very well that he has you at a disadvantage. There's nothing like rage to cloud the thinking process.

Don't give your opponent the satisfaction of knowing he's got you angry and frazzled.

Instead, speak from a position of strength. Stand in your power, marshal all your inner resources and respond calmly and maturely:

"I see you feel there's a point we need to discuss,"
> or,

"I think I understand what you're getting at here."

Annoy the Hell Out of Your Opponent

There are two interesting results: first, if you keep your composure and speak dispassionately, but with inner strength, it drives your opponent crazy—you know, the one who has just spent the whole last hour, day or week working up a case against you.

That person is likely to become even more frustrated in the face of your mature response. You've just cheated him out of a chance to use all this pent-up emotion to blast you back into your place, which would have given him great satisfaction.

The second result is that, as your opponent increases his anger against you, his power diminishes. You have knocked him off balance. Your reasoned response was entirely unexpected and, oh, so annoying!

He may continue to lob verbal pot shots your way, but any barbs he shows in the midst of this frustration will not be well thought out or sent with careful aim.

The Power of Whispers

I started my career life as an elementary school teacher, before moving in another direction. But still today, I have retained a few gems of wisdom from my teaching days. One involves whispers.

Do you realize that it's easier to calm a room full of rowdy school children with whispers, rather than yelling? What an amazing fact! (It works for barking dogs, too!)

The minute you escalate your voice, you join the multitude in a regular free-for-all, and if you've ever been in a room full of children, you quickly discover it's virtually impossible to outshout them.

Whispers, on the other hand, get everyone's attention. What am I missing?? What did I not hear while I was being rowdy??

If dogs are barking and you raise your voice, they think you're joining the pack. If everyone escalates the noise level, we all need to go even higher.

It's exactly the same with arguments—and control is even easier. If you ramp up the noise level, it will be a loud debate all around. You'll expend so much energy in shouting and outdoing your opponent, the finer points will be lost and the result will be chaos.

You have control over the noise level of your arguments. If your opponent tries to escalate the ferociousness of the dispute, you have the power to bring it right back down. And that power is in the form of a whisper. Nobody can stand missing what's said, or at least not for long.

So if you lower your voice to normal speaking level or even lower, you will definitely control the tone of your argument. Your opponent will soon lower his voice to a range that matches yours, because if he doesn't he's apt to miss something.

Try this technique in normal conversation and you'll be amazed the influence you have! In an argument, that influence is not only on volume, but also on anger levels.

Anger rises with volume and volume rises with anger.

Think of how very difficult it is to be enraged when you're speaking in low voices!

> Does whispering ever work well!! I just stopped reading and tried it out on my fiancé, Jake, and his dog, Melvin. I'm laughing, because it worked so well on both of them at the same time!
>
> They both stopped romping and tried to hear what I was saying. They were so sure I was saying something they ought to hear, when actually I was just saying whatever came into my head.
>
> This is great! I would love to have more control over my life. I see women who have everything so well put together—they look and sound self-confident.
>
> I hope by the time I'm their age, I have that element of serenity. And I think the answer is control.

Chapter 6: First One Who Ramps It Up Loses

> Feeling strong and knowing that you're capable and powerful is so important. That's why I love the techniques for feeling my core of inner strength and taking control over situations involving arguments.

Rage-Junkies on an Adrenalin Rush

A surge of adrenalin is so addictive! Rage-Junkies thrive on the stuff. You've met them, I'm sure. Every argument is a World War. And every day needs at least one such confrontation. How annoying to have to put up with one of these types, especially when you're in the line of fire.

When you live or work with a Rage-Junkie, it's very tempting to join in the screaming match. No wonder they talk about arguments clearing the air—relief from the screaming when it's over is what actually clears the air, the blissful peace that follows, when there's a Rage-Junkie involved.

Although these are extreme people, they didn't get to this level of rage overnight. And you can't cure them simply by reading a book. But you can exert control over your arguments by using the techniques I've been explaining.

Life with a Rage-Junkie feels like trying to meditate at 80 mph on a Los Angeles freeway.

With a Rage-Junkie, you'll need to work overtime on mastering the techniques for staying in control, including buying yourself some time, standing in your power, using a quiet yet assertive voice, avoiding confrontational phrases, and learning whispering skills.

Rage (and the need for adrenalin) is partly an ingrained habit. You may never see perfect results, but you should certainly see improvement.

Always remember, quiet and mature shock the heck out of people who expect a rampage. You'll find this to be an easy way to maintain control or to bring the focus back to the actual dispute.

7

Don't Like Your Opponent's Arguments? Rewrite!

You've just spent time listening to whatever your opponent has dished out. The next step toward a win is to rewrite all of the nasty or error-filled statements he or she has made. It's time to start setting the record straight. (See? I said you'd have your day in court!)

First, you need to be certain that you understand exactly what your opponent's position is, and certainly you've been listening to it without rebuttal for what seems like far, far too long. So that's our starting point.

What we'll be rewriting are your opponent's arguments, morphing them from what he said into what you believe to be true, preferably without him realizing a transition has even taken place.

And what's even better, we're going to morph them into something he can also believe to be true!

Because, by the time you're finished, what you believe and what he believes should be the same. Sounds fair enough to me, and I'd imagine to you, too!

The Magic of Morphing

So let's take a sample argument and and I'll show you how it can be morphed from your opponent's version into a place of common understanding (i.e. your position!) We do it in gradual stages. The further apart your positions are, the more rewriting will be required.

Here's an argument. Your husband says: "You're lazy and weak on discipline, and you let the kids get away with murder." Whew! Of course you're not going to agree to that! Your first inclination is either to defend yourself or to accuse him of equally dire deeds.

But if you've been reading this book, you don't do either of those. You follow with the gamut questions outlined in Chapter 5. When he's used up his entire quiver of arrows—when you've learned his entire argument against you—you're ready to morph, through the magic process of rewriting.

Chapter 7: Don't Like Your Opponent's Arguments? Rewrite!

Here's how to start. First we'll study his basic accusation and remove any word that's inflammatory or extremely inaccurate—something you don't want to hear. In this case, we'll lop off "lazy," "weak," and "murder."

Let's see what we have left, and we'll try to reconfigure that sentence using less venomous words and ideas—and we're even going to even give him credit! Notice that you're still validating his concerns. Here's what you come up with:

"I want to make sure I understand your thoughts here—you're concerned that the children are at times not following house rules and if so, could grow up lacking a sense of responsibility?" Then you add, "By the way, I definitely share those concerns!"

But think about what concerns you just agreed to share! Not his original charge, that you're lazy, weak, and basically a total failure as a parent. Instead, you've agreed to a generic statement that most of us would find hard to dispute—that if children grow up without some requirement to abide by rules, they will grow up lacking responsibility.

Where's the part about you being weak and lazy? It got kicked to the curb. This rewriting technique works amazingly well. You'd be surprised at the number of people who will agree to a statement that seems universally acceptable, even though it's a far cry from their first accusations.

Keep this in mind about those first accusations—if your opponent has been stewing up an argument as a surprise for you, by the time the argument is voiced, it's likely to have been worked on for a considerable time, with anger rising and the words becoming increasingly toxic.

Initial accusations are often well rehearsed and designed for maximum impact. That's why they're easy for you to tone down with a rewrite.

Good Lead-ins for a Rewrite

The beginning sentence of a re-write is very important, because it acknowledges and validates your opponent's concern. It should be a little tentative, as though you're evaluating all that you've just heard from your opponent. Here are some samples:

- I want to be sure I understand your concerns…
- I see. So what you're primarily concerned about is ……..
- It's good that you and I both seem to be concerned that….

Notice the tone is not at all belligerent or over-confident. It responds to your opponent's concerns and flatters him that you are taking this seriously.

Great Expectations

In the example we just looked at, the rewrite of the initial accusation was something both parties might agree to, in which case, the argument could be almost over and you'd be able to chalk it up as a win.

However, most arguments take many rewrites to produce clear results on all major points. And not all instigators will readily accept the first rewrite. Some will continue to argue their point.

Let's look at an example of an argument that's fairly difficult to rewrite. We'll go back to the sample accusation where your boss told you that you have no work ethic. After your subsequent questioning, she's added even more: that you are unskilled on the computer and that you have difficulty working with fellow employees.

This is such a mixed bag of accusations, and you're likely to have trouble addressing all of these in your rewrite. Don't even try. If you attempt that, you'll end up arguing each of her points and defending your honor. The argument will escalate out of control until you get fired, which probably won't take long.

So instead, do a rewrite on just one important point, and in this argument you might choose to rewrite the accusation that you don't cooperate with your co-workers. Your rewrite might go like this:

"I'm glad to hear you mention that the strength of a company depends upon team work, because the team in our department is excellent, and it's a great pleasure to be working with and learning from such competent people."

What have you just done? You've acknowledged

your boss's complaint and said that you agree that it's important to the company that you all work as a team. You complimented the team and you have nicely included yourself as a part of it. Congratulations!

> "A woman with a voice is by definition a strong woman. But the search to find that voice can be remarkably difficult."
>
> Melinda Gates

Not Necessarily A Slam-Dunk

Your boss may swallow this nicely, but chances are good she'll realize that you haven't addressed the other two issues. And she may even point out that the team is indeed excellent, but you aren't.

So what do you do then? You do one of two things, you go back to rewrite mode and try again, or you ask more questions. Your second rewrite could go something like this:

"Let me see if I understand your concerns correctly, you feel that while individual initiative is welcome, it's essential to pull together as a team for effective production."

Who can possibly dispute that? And you realize, of course, that while you are striving to understand your boss's concerns (or at least giving that impression) you are still not admitting your weaknesses, although in this response, you have explored the possibility of individual work rather than group effort. However, you've said it in such a way as to have it sound part of a perfectly normal job process.

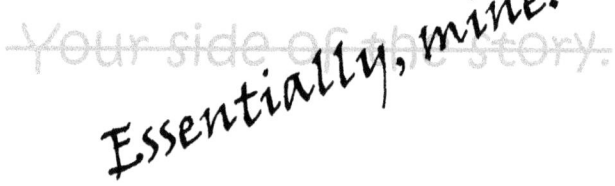

~~Your side of the story.~~ Essentially, mine.

Fall-back Position: More Questions

You can always return to the question mode, or you can combine questions with rewriting:

"Would it be correct to say that you have some concern over the production levels achieved by our team?"

Just be careful that you're keeping the questions within the confines of the argument, in a fairly generalized way. You're still tying yourself to the team, because it's pretty obvious she approves of your fellow team members. Don't separate yourself out from the multitude here. There is safety in numbers.

Questions allow you to vary your rewrites, but they are more difficult, because they appear to ask for a response.

The Argument-Stopper Variation

I want to be sure you have a full range of techniques at your disposal, so now we'll look at a rewrite variation that starts with our magic argument stopper.

In Chapter 3, I taught you how to stop an argument on a dime—instantly and effectively. Of course, stopping an argument is not winning, but it's a very handy technique that allows you not to have to engage in an argument that cannot be won.

The technique was simply to respond to the opening salvo with the words, "You're right," or some variation on that theme. So if your goal is to end or prevent an argument, stop right there. That's quite sufficient, without adding any additional thoughts. In fact, if you do say anything more, you'll be opening yourself up to additional arguing.

However, you can use those same words, even if you want the argument to continue. In that case, you'll want to follow them with a rewrite of the accusation. Let's check that out by going back to the family argument:

"You're lazy and weak on discipline, and you let the kids get away with murder."

Using the argument-stopper with a rewrite, your response might be:

"You're right. Children do need a framework of rules so they can grow up responsibly. I think we're both in agreement on that."

Again, his "lazy and weak" allegation somehow got edited out, right into the trash bin. You have managed to rewrite the meat of the argument, without implicating yourself or your children.

People love to hear the words, "You're right!" Love it so much that the argument is often over by the time you've finished the rewrite.

Chapter 7: Don't Like Your Opponent's Arguments? Rewrite!

" Have you noticed that some people have a hard time telling other people they're right. They stand on principle and can't seem to get those words out, even to save themselves from a crazy argument. I can see where people like that would choke on the words, "You're right."

But if what they're referring to isn't the original accusation or any part of it, and instead is a completely rewritten argument that both people can agree with, "You're right," isn't hard at all! "

Take A Tip From Michelangelo

Depending upon the persistence of your opponent and the complexity of the argument, you may have to rewrite several times.

Think of it like Michelangelo carving the Pietà. Chip a little off one side, hack some off the other side and a bit off the back, until eventually the sculpture takes shape. That is exactly how an argument is won.

History likely didn't preserve Michelangelo's first attempt at sculpture, but we can assume that he improved his skills with practice. It's exactly the same with your arguments.

Practice does indeed allow you to hone your techniques, to the point where you may develop marketable skill in negotiating, which after all is simply arguing with a classy name.

But since no one wants to be a one-trick pony, keep reading. As you read about more techniques, you'll find other ways to chip away at an argument.

8

The Body Language of Arguments

When you're in the middle of an argument, how can you tell if you're winning?

Like an intrepid explorer, you need to look for clues that can help you judge your position. There's no GPS or compass to help point the way, and no pedometer to tell how far you've come. But that doesn't mean you're out of resources.

To gauge your progress, the tools you'll need are observation, intuition and a basic knowledge of arguing styles.

You Say To-may-to, I Say To-mah-to

For all our talk of equality—and indeed both men and women can be superb arguers, debaters and negotiators—in the realm of argument, equality does not mean similarity. The differences between the genders in this arena are vast.

Since I'm a woman whose career choice results in a virtual membership to what I consider a "Boys' Club," where fewer than 20% of my counterparts are women, I've had plenty of opportunity to watch men discuss and debate issues.

What a difference! These dissimilarities occur in every part of the argument, including choice of words, method of delivery and body language.

But you knew all that, I'm sure, just from having arguments with men!

Why the Sexes Argue As They Do

Even if you're planning to restrict your arguments to women only (Ha! As if that could ever happen!), it's a good idea to study what both genders do. You'll pick up some tips you might not have considered.

No one would deny that men, as a whole, have an edge on aggression. They grow up this way from childhood. Physical size is one reason, but cultural lessons are another.

Men use aggressive words and gestures. They are usually direct and committed to winning. Women, on the other hand, are more verbally attuned.

Chapter 8: The Body Language of Arguments

We prefer to win our disputes with words rather than fists. We also allow ourselves a full range of emotions, and we don't hesitate to bring the power of emotions into our language when we speak. Of course some women are aggressive, but usually they don't major in it.

Historically, women have been the property of men—Alpha men, the leaders of the pack. Just as we train our dogs to heel, sit and fetch on command, over the centuries in most cultures women have likewise been trained not to grab the biggest hunk of meat, not to express opinions, and not to put their needs and desires first—and even not to have needs and desires.

Of course this is changing. Women today have greater individual rights, power and freedom than their counterparts of a hundred years ago, or even fifty. They are seeking better education, obtaining higher levels of employment, and should be earning wages equal to that of men.

But still they argue differently. That's why this book is for you, for women only, not for your husband, father, boyfriend or brother. This formula for winning is not for them, because they play by a different set of rules. In other words, their basic arguing style is different.

> "Reginald, why don't you ever let me wi-in?"
> "Because, my tenderness, it's simply never done."
>
> Jane Evers

Even today, women have to learn to feel confident that they will win, and to insist on it. They have to teach themselves not to pull their punches. They need to be direct, but not aggressive.

We Don't Need Aggression

Aggression is detrimental to arguments, and so men often find themselves at a disadvantage because of that, especially if they've so far relied on force to bully their way to a conclusion. While women, in general, need to learn to become more assertive, men, in general, need to learn how to tone their aggression down.

I truly think women definitely have an edge on "savvy" and "canny," and they are sensitive to the clues used to determine progress in an argument.

Chapter 8: The Body Language of Arguments

Their language edge also gives them a better ability to rewrite those arguments to fit their viewpoint.

It sometimes happens that women drift over to the dark side, borrowing aggression from their male opponents and preparing a blast to level the entire city, when a well-thought-out chess move would win the game.

Just remember that women don't have to go there, even when arguing with men, and it reduces our effectiveness when we do.

Standing in your power, the technique we talked about in Chapter 4, is a way to become more comfortable with assertiveness, and I would recommend that you review that section. What often works well for women is a quiet inner force, where the core of your body feels a measure of strength. If you learn to project this aura, your arguments will be automatically strengthened.

> "Women don't realize how powerful they are."
>
> Judith Light

The Body Language of Arguments

The beginning stage of an argument usually involves aggression, anger or frustration on the part of the instigator. After all, why argue if you're not angry or frustrated! So this individual will be giving clues to as to motive, emotions and intensity in his or her body language.

A savvy woman analyzes these as the argument gets underway. The more exaggerated the gesture or movement, and the faster the speed, or the more sudden or sexually oriented, the more intense the emotion.

Clues to Aggression or Anger

- Suddenly invading your bubble—moving closer than is comfortable
- Sneering, frowning, staring intently
- Rude or angry gestures, such as clenched fists, attack stance
- Aggressive or dominant touching (even an arm around the shoulders)
- Flushed face, rapid breathing

Clues to Frustration

- Sighs of exasperation

- Gestures of helplessness (arms thrown down)
- Look of disapproval and dismay
- Pacing
- Running hands through the hair

This is certainly not a complete list, but it gives you an idea of what kind of body language to look for.

Clues during the Gambit Phase

In this phase of the argument, you're asking questions, and you will continue to do so until you have determined the extent of your opponent's case against you. Observing body and oral language can help you know when you've reached the end of that stage, and are ready to rewrite your opponent's arguments. In the Gambit, when you're nearing the end of that stage, look for:

- Hesitation before answers
- Confusion or stuttering
- Repetition
- Frustration that becomes more apparent (we just covered those clues)

If any of these become obvious, you're hitting a nerve. And, it's time to start rewriting the arguments.

Signs that You're Winning

During the Rewrite phase, an opponent's body language can tell you if your rewrite is on the right track. Watch your opponent for these submissive signs:

- Sits down, leans back
- Lowers the head
- Unwraps arms that were folded across chest
- Holds hands out, palms up
- Slower, smaller more open gestures

Look like a Winner!

Here are the body language signs that you'll want to practice, to send the message to your opponent that you are confident in your ability to win:

- Hold your body still, with no fidgeting or anxious moves
- Keep your head upright and still, with no rapid eye movements
- If you're sitting, lean back in your chair with your arms open
- Your shoulders should be down and back
- Your movements are slower, very natural and relaxed

Now don't you feel like winning? Follow those suggestions and you'll be on the right track.

A Word about Eye Contact

You've no doubt heard the adage that eye contact is essential in business, especially in sales. (And actually, arguments are a form of sales—you're selling your opinion to your opponent.) Eye contact has long been believed to demonstrate sincerity, honesty, fortitude, perseverance and all sorts of other presidential qualities.

All of that was considered factual. But a September 2013 article in Psychological Science, a journal of the Association of Psychological Science, burst that bubble with a research study confirming that eye contact does not promote persuasion, as generations of salespeople have been taught.

This study showed that during persuasive situations, maintaining direct eye contact causes the recipient to resist changing his or her attitude.

Steady eye contact can also be viewed as confrontational or aggressive. If you look back at our list of aggressive tendencies, you'll see that "staring intently" is a sign of aggression.

So be careful with your eye contact if you want to avoid aggressiveness. Keep your eye movements natural and make eye contact frequently but without fixing the stare on an opponent whose opinions you want to sway.

While you're making your point persuasively through a rewrite, glance down or away as you drive it home. That way it'll be met with less resistance and will have a better chance of acceptance.

Reetha

> Slip it to 'em, baby! I have no tolerance for aggressive men—throwbacks to the Stone Age. So it's good to have a saner, more intelligent arguing style given credence.
>
> It's amazing to me that some men still think they can dominate women and arguments—

the condescending pat on the shoulder and the basic assumption that might is right. What happens if we're louder than men? We just get labeled "bitches." So let's not even go there.

Instead of being louder, I'd much rather be smarter, and win that way. We can do it. We've got what it takes to be verbally powerful. And I know we've got what it takes to win.

Girls, don't you find aggression so passé? And incredibly tiresome. When are guys going to get the message? Probably when we know how to win. 🙶

So What's Wrong with Aggression?

The argument could be made that women should fight fire with fire. If we interact with men frequently, in business or social circles, shouldn't we adopt their style of argument? My response to that is, why would you ever want to do that?

Aggression is simply not necessary for winning an argument, even if your opponent is a bully. Or maybe I should say, especially if your opponent is a bully. The most effective way to counteract bully behavior is not to scream, or rant, or pile on the aggressive body language. That simply escalates the argument.

How to Influence An Aggressive Opponent

Instead, follow the principle of Whispering I talked about in Chapter 6. Lower your voice and calm your movements. But be sure to maintain your position of power with strong body language. It's amazing how much influence you can have on an aggressive opponent simply by being assertive but non-aggressive.

And consider this: aggressive people dominate through force. They haven't mastered the art of negotiation or they wouldn't be carrying out less-than-productive bullying. So be confident that your argument style will not be challenged. After all, bullies don't practice Gambit questions and Rewriting. But you have! And your confidence can and will carry the day.

The next chapter will give you more techniques for winning arguments, to add to your basic Gambit-Rewrite scenario. So far our arguments are pretty skinny and they still need to be beefed up with facts, statistics and guest appearances.

9

Beef Up Your Argument

Facts should never be used as a club, to knock your opponent senseless. Instead, think of them as the mortar that holds your argument together.

Who looks at a building and says, "Great mortar there!" You'd have to be a bricklayer to get turned on by what's holding it together. It's exactly the same with facts in an argument. They should be inconspicuous, yet essential. They support your opinions and tie the argument into a unified whole.

Even though—when you're first faced with an accusation from your opponent—you have an almost irresistible tendency to defend yourself and slather your rebuttal with facts, don't do it!

Resist the temptation and ask your Gambit questions, exactly as outlined in Chapter 5.

When you move into the Rewrite phase, in the beginning of that stage avoid adding any facts. But if the first rewrite or two aren't sufficient to make progress or end the argument, you can certainly start introducing a few facts, but only with great care.

Stay Away From Facts You Can't Swear By

It's pretty obvious to most of us that facts are facts. They are so black and white, and cut and dried, that they are either facts or not.

> "She climbed up the argument ahead of me, getting toeholds on what she called 'facts.' Ha! I knew every one of those 'facts' was there just to roll down and knock me off."
>
> Therese Duchamp

If something can't be verified, it's not a fact, so don't use it. You may get away with using phony "facts" a time or two, when your opponent doesn't take time to verify. But in the long run, you lose face and reputation, and it just isn't worth arguing dishonestly.

If you feel you have to present a statement but aren't sure it's factual, be truthful to your opponent. Say, "I'm not certain this is true, but I've heard that…."

How to Slip in a Fact

The best way to slip in a fact is to do it almost under the radar, in a very unassuming spot.

For example, in our argument about your performance on the job, you were accused by your boss of having poor computer skills, no work ethic and a lack of team effort. It's a fact that you've registered to take a course in Word Processing 101, and when the accusation is first voiced, it's very tempting to say something like:

"Really, my job performance is great and I'll have you know that I signed up for Word Processing 101, not because I needed it but just to keep up my skills." Ooh, bad!

And even if you just said, in your defense: "Well, I just signed up for Word Processing 101," that bold-faced fact is sitting there by itself, waiting for a challenge from your boss, which could go something like this: "You've been working here for two years and haven't had the initiative until now to improve your skills."

But if you slip your fact in with other comments, it's less likely to be challenged, and yet it assumes a supporting role. So instead, try this for one of your rewrites:

"I'm glad this is a company that's concerned about team effort, and I'm so fortunate to be on a wonderful team. They inspired me to go back to college in the evening to take an additional course in Word Processing."

So what's good about this one? First of all, there's acknowledgment and validation of the boss's concerns. Praise for the company and team.

You included yourself on the team—stuck there like glue (maybe they won't fire you)—and you sneaked in the fact that you were "inspired" toward better performance (without actually saying it). You actually made it sound like the team is working well. So with luck, your boss may discover her arguments aren't valid after all.

What if You're Ratted Out?

But what if the team members actually don't work together well, and someone ratted you out because she doesn't like you?

You could rewrite the accusation something like this:

"I'm glad this is a company that's not only concerned about team effort, but also appreciates individual performance. I'm so fortunate to be working here. This has inspired me to go back to college in the evening to take an additional course in Word Processing."

Do you bring up complaints that the team is lousy and this is the reason for your failure as an employee? Nope. Stay as far as you can away from mentioning weaknesses of any sort—yours or the team's.

Save your complaints about the team for a later date, when you're securely back in the company fold. You need to solve your own work problems first.

" My first job after college was in a place where the morale was horrible. There were awful arguments during staff meetings, many of which were the result of one employee ratting on another.

It was the most unpleasant place I've ever worked. The strange thing was, we were all mental health counselors, and we couldn't even sail a clean ship! How could we possibly help our patients if we were so ill-equipped to achieve resolution on our own issues!

I wish I'd had this book back then, but fortunately new management introduced a couple of the techniques you've mentioned here, and gradually we developed better team habits.

It's amazing, but when people are able to handle arguments in the workplace more effectively, there end up being fewer of them. "

Statistics Are Facts with Numbers Attached

Depending on the subject of your argument, statistics can work well to add weight to your words. Just don't sound like you're trying to be the smartest kid in the class, a show-off for sure!

Going back to our argument with your husband that you're a lazy, unfit parent who lets her kids run wild, you might use a statistic or two in those rewrites.

One might go something like this:

"I see we both understand the need to raise children who take responsibility for their actions. I've read that children are 80% more likely to lead a happy life, free from depression, if they have been encouraged to be responsible for their toys. I'm sure you'll agree that's something we both should emphasize."

> "Be able to analyze statistics, which can be used to support or undercut almost any argument."
>
> Marilyn vos Savant

This argument is actually negotiation in process, and I have no doubt that it will be resolved to both people's satisfaction.

Gone are the inflammatory words like, lazy and wild. And in their place will be, by the time the argument is over, a mature and responsible solution.

Get Some Extra Help!

If you need extra help in stating your case, you can certainly quote an authority. Again, it's much better to slip it in, almost as an afterthought.

If you're going to quote someone, be darn sure the quote fits and is actually helping. If you come out of the blue with a pronouncement that doesn't quite do the job, it can set you back considerably.

For the workplace argument, avoid something like this: "As Princess Diana once said, 'People think at the end of the day that a man is the only answer to fulfillment. Actually a job is better for me.' And I agree with her."

Not a horrible quote—it could have been worse—but it doesn't earn you any bonus points. Why did you say it? This isn't the quote that's going to keep your job for you. Instead, you may be looked on as an odd duck, not exactly team material.

If you're going to lean on a quotation, take time to cite an appropriate authority and work the quote in well, even if you have to paraphrase it, so it has real meaning Here's a good example of a rewrite with a quote (and this one's actually a statistic too):

"I agree that good work skills are vitally important, and I was pleased to hear our company chairman announce that two thirds of our firm's work force has had some college experience. I was inspired enough to register for a word processing class."

You're like greased lightning, girl! No one's going to stop you with a statement like that. Your boss didn't actually say that good work skills are important, but obviously she thinks it, because she criticized yours. So essentially you're giving her a statement that you know she can agree with.

Agreement is such a big issue in arguments that we're going to devote the whole next chapter to the subject. In an argument, reaching an agreement is exactly what you want. So let's go get it!

10

Get Ready to Nail That Agreement

You can't have a win without agreement, so now it's time to lock that in agreement. Are you ready?

By now, you've mastered both the Gambit and the Rewrite, and you've enriched your argument with various other techniques. With luck and lots of practice, you've may have even reached a consensus with your opponent, or at least a partial agreement. So nailing a win won't be difficult.

If your rewrites haven't produced agreement on anything, read this chapter and then try a few more rewrites.

With an opponent who is argumentative, stubborn and unwilling to agree to anything, the job can be quite difficult. Some individuals are unwilling to see reason no matter what. Although this can certainly cause you problems, you have to realize that even the most skilled negotiator could fail to reach accord. (Look at the Israelis and Palestinians if you want to see a tough negotiation situation.) Not every argument has a happy ending. But I want to give you a formula to insure that most of yours will.

A Fresh Set of Arguments

Let's start with a whole new set of arguments, because we've worked our old ones to death. Your opponent leads off with his argument (*in italics*), while your unspoken position on each issue is shown below:

1. *"Your idea of buying a condo in the downtown area stinks."*
   I'd love to move downtown, away from the suburbs.

2. *"You let the kids be obnoxious at bedtime and they're like zombies in the morning."*
   I wish he'd help me get them to bed. Doesn't he realize I have work too?

3. *"I'm going to the bar whenever I want and there's nothing you can do about it."*

Chapter 10: Get Ready to Nail That Agreement

I like going out with him on the weekends, but I wish he'd stay home weeknights.

4. *"There's no way your irritating mother's coming here for a visit."*

   I only get to see Mom twice a year. If his mother gets to visit, mine can too.

5. *"Absolutely...No...New...Car! Are you crazy?"*

   I deserve a new car since he got one last year.

There you have them—five new arguments to practice on. We'll work on the rewrites, concentrating on securing an agreement from your opponent.

Don't worry whether or not it's the right agreement at this point. Start your rewrites in very general terms:

1. I think it's great that you and I both are so conscientious about our world's resources.

2. I know that we both love children.

3. From what you're saying, it seems we both enjoy getting together with our friends.

4. I think we both can say that we're supportive of each other emotionally.

5. We both can agree that new cars smell wonderful.

Generalized rewrites are a good way to change an argumentative mood into a congenial one. After all, who's arguing here? You're both in agreement. However, it isn't sufficient agreement to be considered a win, because the statement doesn't get to the meat of the dispute.

But that's okay, because we're taking it a step at a time. If your opponent agrees with those generalized statements, you can move on to more detailed rewrites, such as:

1. I think we can agree that our petroleum resources are limited.

2. I'm sure you'd agree that it's wise to get toddlers in bed before midnight.

3. Do you agree that going out to bars on weeknights makes it difficult to get up for work?

Chapter 10: Get Ready to Nail That Agreement

4. I'd say one thing we can agree on is that family unity is important.
5. I'm sure we'd both love a new car if there were a way to afford it.

You can probably guess where these are heading! Yes, indeed: a condo downtown, more help at toddler bedtime, an agreement on more home time during the week, a visit from a mother- in-law and a new car.

Continue to increase the detail with statements that indicate you're both in agreement so far. If you reach a stalling point, go back a little and do a more generalized rewrite.

Difficulties? Take a Little Bite out of It

If, in your rewrites, you can't find common ground—a statement that you both can agree on—break it down into tiny sound bites. Or take a detour:

1. Parking next to our office is getting so expensive, isn't it?
2. We're lucky, aren't we, that young Ian and Emma are such happy kids.
3. I know that we both love country music.

4. Oh…we both know my mother makes the best apple pie!
  5. I think we agree that leather is a little more durable than cloth for kids.

You can always head back to the main issue, so don't be afraid of detours.

Make YES a Habit

See what's happening? You're making it easy for your opponent to say, "Yes." And Yes is on the way to a win!

Yes, yes, yes becomes a habit that is easy to continue. Training for sales reps use this technique because it actually works. Focusing your opponent's attention on the positive will shift the negative thoughts and reactions from his mind.

If a person answers, "Yes," to ten questions in a row, saying, "No," to the eleventh is not so easy. He or she has begun to develop a habit of saying, "Yes."

You know how hard it is to break habits! Put this idea to work for you.

Chapter 10: Get Ready to Nail That Agreement

> This is like the game kids play, getting you used to answering a single word time and time again, then changing it with the last question.
>
> You give the same answer ten times and on the eleventh, something has changed, and you end up giving an answer that suddenly doesn't fit the question.
>
> You usually discover, however, that the little darlings have tricked you into saying a forbidden potty word!

Yes, it's very much like that, although it's not as simplistic as the children's game, and it's not a trick.

The same technique is used in negotiations all around the world. Find generalized common ground you can agree on and work your way around an issue until you've reached a consensus. If you come to a roadblock, approach it from another direction.

Just keep finding areas in which you can agree. If you can't find major areas, find the tiny ones first. You will eventually get there.

Agree to Time Out

If you reach an impasse in your argument or tempers start to rise, agree to take a time out. But before you leave the table, set a schedule for resuming your discussion. That's what governments do in the middle of a public hearing, they are allowed to "continue the deliberation to a date and time specific," and that's what they do, they set the date and time to pick it back up again.

That makes it official, and gives your argument the respect it deserves.

Total Agreement Isn't Necessary

Many arguments are concluded—even "won"—without total agreement on both sides. That's perfectly fine if both parties are satisfied with the results.

Chapter 10: Get Ready to Nail That Agreement

Usually, you and your opponent start miles apart in your demands, and you each may have pumped up your list because you figure you'll end up with only about half of what's on it. So you aim high, but say you'd be happy with less.

That's human nature and everyone accepts the fact that this is how negotiation works. However, it frequently happens that one party will "forget" that the list is inflated, and all of a sudden every item on that list becomes non-negotiable.

This usually happens when tempers rage and neither party has made an effort to calm the waters. Demands become ridiculous when emotions run high.

Don't let that happen to your argument! Use the calming techniques, such as Whispering and Gambit questions, to keep your debate on track.

And aim for the quickest, best agreement you can get.

Give & Take

Sometimes if you're willing to give an inch, you'll get a mile. Just like the inflated list of demands I mentioned, there are times when you can afford to be generous to your opponent, without being a wimp, rolling over or wearing a sign that reads "Tromp on me."

You should use the negotiable items on your list of demands as bargaining chips, but how you do it will determine your overall success. Never offer to bargain in the standard way or, sure as shootin', you'll lose. Don't say, "I'll do this, if you do that for me."

Instead, wait for the moment to arise when a truly diplomatic gesture is called for. Perhaps you've come to an impasse. This is when you magnanimously and graciously give one of those bargaining chips to the other party.

Don't bargain or demand an equal gift in return, and don't make your offer too early in the game, or you'll look desperate. Shock the heck out of your opponent with your generous nature when it makes you look good.

You knew it was negotiable anyway. You'll have just given an inch, but it's almost certain that you'll get more in return than you would have if you'd bargained.

Ask for the "Sale"

This step can be so very difficult for some people, but as you practice, it gets easier. If you attended a training class to be a sales rep, you'd have this message drummed into you: You must always ask for the sale!

What it means, is that you *must* close the deal, and an argument is exactly like a sale. If you were selling a new car to a customer, you'd follow much of the same formula I've talked about in this book. You'd gradually suggest questions and rewrites that commit the customer emotionally, step by step:

- "Wouldn't an SUV work well for your children and dogs?"
- "I think you can agree that 40 miles per gallon is excellent for a family vehicle."

- "Do you think that leather seats would be practical for your family and pets?"
- "Wouldn't you agree that Pacific Blue is a wonderful rich color?"
- "I think we can all imagine your family enjoying a trip to the beach in this SUV!"

Of course I've left some steps out here, but you see the trend. When the customer, Ms. Smith, agrees to the last rewrite, you close the sale, "Let's go jot down some numbers and see if it works for you."

At that point, I can pretty much guarantee it—you're buying a new car!

Arguments are essentially the same. ***You must close the deal.*** When you feel you're as close as you're going to get to a consensus, your final rewrite is going to nail it.

11

The Win

Winning an argument isn't a matter of total destruction of the other side. Instead, it's the process of bringing closure to an issue that's a sore point. Often you can't change an opponent's deep seated beliefs. However, you can learn how to give that person the validation she needs to make her feel she's made her statement, and to make her comfortable in supporting your position.

She may not score a single "point," but she'll leave the confrontation feeling okay about it.

Chocolate's Not Meant to Be Gulped

If you're skillful—and incredibly lucky—you've managed to nab a win early in the Rewrite stage. But no matter how much skill you've acquired, it would still take a dose of luck to win after only a couple of rounds.

And, let's face it, you may not want to win quite so quickly, even if you could. Two reasons here, first, a victory after a tough, well-played game (or argument) can be a lot more satisfying to the winner than facing an opponent who rolls over in defeat at the opening salvo.

Savor your Victory!

The difference between swallowing a mocha truffle in one gulp vs. appreciating it in tiny bites. Savoring your victory is so much more fun!

And second, it would be to your benefit to let your opponent feel that she's played a good game. For the defeated team, losing by only two points results in a loss that's disappointing, as opposed to a 40-0 skunking that's devastating to morale. With a close and well-played game, the losing team members leave the field knowing that they put up a good opposition, instead of slinking off, crushed, angry and defeated.

When people aren't allowed to save face after an argument, vengeance takes hold. And if you're the winner, unless you're a masochist who enjoys repeat arguments, you don't want to go there!

Chapter 11: The Win

Wrap It Up And Add A Bow

During the course of your argument you've been rewriting and rewriting so hard, you might even end up rewriting your dreams. But those rewrites have brought you closer to your ultimate goal.

It may not have always been a straight path. If you ran into resistance, you may have had to take small detours around a sticking point, or even to go back to using generalities and try again.

Gradually you've narrowed down your opponent's arguments, winnowed the wheat from the chaff, and zeroed on the real complaint, which is sometimes surprisingly tiny.

And it's almost always smaller in size and intensity than the initial argument your opponent started out with.

After establishing what the real issue is, by rewriting you've gotten him or her to agree on lots of small points: yes, he can agree that it's expensive to have to park downtown; yes, she can agree that your registration in Word Processing 101 shows initiative; and yes, he can agree that children are much better behaved when well rested.

By now you've taken control of the argument and reshaped it into something that's no longer an argument, but something both of you can agree on.

It's important to finalize the results, so that both parties will feel that the issue has been brought to a close, even though in reality, your accuser did not get what he or she originally asked for.

As you've pared it down in the rewrites—roped the argument and hauled in the lasso—you've done it so gradually and skillfully your opponent may have no idea that you're about to win the rodeo!

You may have made a concession on a minor point (one of your negotiables)—through strategic choice, not necessity. But your basic position is intact.

Watch your opponent's body language to check for signs that you're winning (we talked about those in Chapter 8). When you're fairly certain your opponent is ready to concede it's time to seal the deal.

Go For It!

A Win is essentially a recap of your position, but done with sensitivity and common sense. It's the final rewrite of the points you both agree on, with some of the supporting details thrown in.

For example, on the argument over buying a downtown condo vs. staying in the suburbs, the recap might go like this:

"It seems as though we're both in agreement that the high cost of gas, the necessity of maintaining two cars, and the nuisance of arriving home tired at 9 pm every night would be resolved by moving downtown."

When your opponent says, "Yes;" the argument is over.

In the case of the argument over the mother-in-law's visit, here's how the recap might sound.

"We both agree that we love each other and want to support each other emotionally, through thick and thin. We both recognize the values of family unity, and moreover, we both want to play by rules that are fair and kind. I do realize that my mom can be irritating to you, and this is something we can agree to discuss further, to find ways to minimize this.

But I think we both agree that in fairness to each of us, we should be allowed one free pass per quarter for a visit from a relative of our choice. Wouldn't you say that's reasonable?"

In either of these situations, if you'd said this at the beginning of the argument (actually you were thinking these very same points, weren't you?) you would have been chopped up and fed by your opponent to the lions. And your opponent's opinion would have remained carved in stone forever.

Instead you played it smart. You roped that bull and let it run off some steam before you hauled it in.

Take a bow, Rodeo Queen! (We will ignore the fact that Rodeo Queens don't actually get to rope bulls—but that's an argument for another day.)

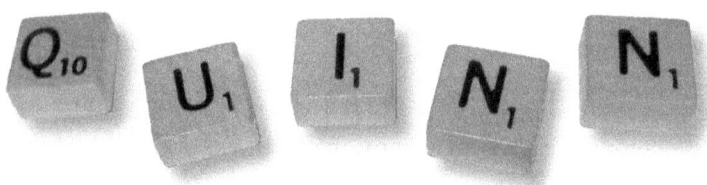

" OMG! Love it! Love it! I always wanted to be Queen of the Rodeo. I sure know where to find plenty of bull, and a lasso's easy enough to come by.

Chapter 11: The Win

> This is definitely gonna work for me. Thanks for the DIY guide to making my dream come true!
>
> I love the control your formula gives me. Haven't had any problem finding arguments, and there's no shortage of pithy comments to make, but I like the way you wrap the arguments up in a neat bundle.
>
> Unfortunately, sometimes I have the habit of reacting far too strongly—blowing my opponent out of the water. But holding back an immediate blast has a certain satisfaction, and no guilt after.
>
> This kind of win definitely feels more pleasing.
>
> Regards,
> Quinn, the newly crowned Rodeo Queen

When a Win Doesn't Feel Like a Win

You can't declare a win unless you have agreement on most—80% or 90%—of your original position. If you've had to concede a major point that leaves you not completely satisfied, it won't feel like a win.

So work hard on the rewrites to shape the argument to your liking. With practice, you can do it.

Never denigrate your opponent. In fact, this is pretty hard to do when you're standing in your power and speaking calmly, but it's a point to keep in mind.

You want to end the argument with an ex-opponent who doesn't feel belittled or vanquished, but who feels that his or her position was understood and respected. And it allows your opponent to feel as though he or she's been a part of the solution.

Shake on It!

I see eyes rolling at the mere thought of shaking hands to seal a resolution. But it's not as ridiculous as you might think.

In certain dispute situations a handshake is a normal ending to discussions. Two ambassadors sign a treaty, they shake hands. So in our culture, a handshake has significance, with the underlying meaning being, "You have my word on this."

The same is true in some business situations: sales, certainly routinely; or after important decisions and discussions at the management level.

Chapter 11: The Win

But in our lower level or informal business discussions, social negotiations or family feuds, we use handshakes rarely if ever. So if we break with tradition and unexpectedly shake hands with our spouse, a co-worker or BFF after an argument, the effect can be electrifying in the most positive way.

Children and teens react very well to a handshake, because that one gesture elevates them to a position of maturity and helps them feel a part of the final decision.

A handshake restores your opponent's dignity and self-worth, and reduces the chances that you'll be back arguing those same issues later. The fact that, in days of yore, women didn't shake hands, makes this an even more powerful and meaningful technique for us.

> **"Argue for the sheer and wonderful joy of it!"**
> Amanda Burns

So you've won and, not only that, you've followed the winning formula and developed an argument style that's now become a good habit.

But wouldn't you love to put these techniques to a wider use? Maybe even earn back the price of this book? Read on!

12

Negotiating For Fun And Profit

When you picked up this book, perhaps you were facing arguments that went nowhere or found yourself on the losing end of every negotiation.

Now that you've learned the formula to winning an argument and honed your skills, you're ready to put your expertise to work in different arenas.

I hope you've tried out the formula in your personal life and have found that arguments are not as devastating or frustrating for you as they once were.

The reason is because now you have a plan to follow and know techniques for keeping yourself in control of the situation, no matter what twists and sneaky tactics are thrown at you.

Don't ever let your opponent get under your skin! You not only have the skills to avoid showing it, you now also have the expertise to sidestep it. Never be afraid to back away from an argument. Avoiding arguments is not a sign of weakness, it's a sign of intelligence.

As you've seen, many arguments are much better left untouched. If someone provokes you with intent to argue, determine if this is an argument that not only needs to be won, but can be won.

It's a fact of life that arguments are everywhere. At work, these newly developed skills will improve your interpersonal relationships, with employees, bosses, clients or customers. They will help you to develop an air of competence, confidence and serenity. The inner strength that helps you win arguments, also gives you a powerful edge in the workplace.

There are plenty of other arenas where your skills are valued. Negotiations take place everywhere, from personal to high-level intergovernment discussions. Somebody has earned good money negotiating between the Israelis and Palestinians, right?

Negotiators use these same skills every day, because negotiation, like an argument, is exactly like fusing together the ends of those two fat cords, seamlessly and invisibly.

Chapter 12: Negotiating for Fun And Profit

Negotiation/argument skills are marketable, so if you're ready to expand your horizons, here are a few opportunities that rely on this expertise:

- Sales—every single kind!
- Dispute Resolution
- Arbitration and Litigation
- Politics
- Counseling
- Business
- Union Reps

Negotiation skills will automatically make you a more valuable employee and a more competent manager. Offer to help settle an office dispute. Become the go-to person when two parties cannot reach an agreement. You'll find that your skills are often welcome, and the more problems you solve, the more your reputation will be enhanced.

Review this formula from time to time to keep your skills in good form. And whether you argue from necessity, for fun or for profit, you'll develop the habit of winning, without being labeled a bitch.

May your arguments be few—unless you're getting paid for them—and your wins satisfying!

Index

A
aggression - 26, 61, 79, 80, 94, 95, 96, 97, 98, 102, 103, 104
anger - 73-80
AnswerGirl comments -
  Brooke - 20
  Emma - 78, 121
  Hannah - 68
  Kristin - 9, 91
  Madison - 30, 110
  Quinn - 132
  Reetha - 39, 102
  Tennyson - 49
arguing skills - 11, 80, 88, 92
arguing style - 26, 74, 75, 76, 77, 93, 96, 104
argument formula - 10, 11, 42, 137
argumentative spouse - 18, 21, 43, 44, 49, 82, 83, 90, 111
assumptions - 41-43
attitude check - 23-34, 67

B
Banks, Bronwyn S. (quote) - 41
bitch label - 8, 9, 10, 73, 103, 139
body language - 93-104, 130
Burns, Amanda (quote) - 135
buying time - 50-55

C
Carter, Rosalynn (quote) - 52
closing moves - 22, 115-126
common group - 121-122
crazy fact arguments - 15-16
crazy-loonies - 37, 45, 73

D
debates & debating - 16, 24, 29, 30, 31, 53, 76
Duchamp, Therese (quote) - 106

E
envy - 19-28, 94, 130
Evans, Victoria (quote) - 36
ending the argument - 43-46, 89, 90
Evers, Jane (quote) - 96
eye contact - 101-102

F
facts - 106-108
false accusations - 36, 59-60, 63, 83, 84
Faulkner, Carin (quote) - 57
first strategic move - 64
Forester, Danielle M. (quote) - 38

G
game plan - 62, 107-108
Gates, Melinda (quote) - 87
good sport arguments - 13-14
ground rules - 33, 47

H
Hetherington, Mary (quote) - 36
Handshake 134-135

I
intellectual arguments - 14-15

J
Jeffers, Joan (quote) - 32, 34

140

Index

L
Light, Judith (quote) - 97
Lindsay, Anne (quote) - 4
losing position - 35, 109

M
mental abuse - 20-21m duties - 11, 12, 13, 14, 15, 16

N
negotiation techniques - 11, 23, 24, 31, 92, 104, 116, 125, 130, 137-39

O
opening gambit - 58, 59-72, 81, 99, 104, 105, 115
opinion arguments - 16-17

P
perennial arguments - 19-20
power points - 105-114
practice techniques - 27-29
psycho-cybernetics - 27, 30, 31

Q
Quotes -
  Banks, Bronwyn S. - 41
  Burns, Amanda - 135
  Carter, Rosalynn - 52
  Duchamp, Therese - 106
  Evers, Jane - 96
  Faulkner, Carin - 57
  Forester, Danielle M. - 38
  Gates, Melinda - 87
  Hetherington, Mary - 36
  Jeffers, Joan - 32, 34
  Light, Judith - 97
  Lindsay, Anne - 4
  Savant, Marilyn vos - 111
  Thatcher, Margaret - 66

R
rage junkies - 79-80
reasons vs expectations - 67

rebuttal - 43, 52, 64, 67, 68, 71, 81, 105
recap - 130
revealing your position - 63, 64, 71
rewrites - 81-92, 97, 99, 100, 102, 104, 106, 108, 113, 115, 117, 118, 119, 127, 129, 130, 134

S
Savant, Marilyn vos (quote) - 111
sincerity - 16, 17, 18
sportsmanship - 26, 32
standing in your power - 51-52, 60, 74, 80, 97, 100, 134
starting point - 81, 123
statistics - 111

T
Thatcher, Margaret (quote) - 66
the agreement - 115, 122-126, 133-135
time and place - 47-58, 60, 79, 80
tired & cranky arguments - 18-19, 49
torpedo arguments - 20-21
types of arguments - 13-22

U
unwinnable arguments - 34, 35-46, 138

V
validation - 62, 63, 84, 85, 108, 127
verbal attacks - 21
victory - 10, 26, 128

W
winnable arguments - 15, 17
winning mindset - 32, 33, 59, 70
winning the argument - 33, 47, 127-136
worst places to argue - 55-58
worst times to argue - 48, 49

141

Follow the AnswerGirls...

and enjoy other titles in this series of books and e-books— as always, by women, for women.

Love 'em?
Please take the time to give us a review on Amazon.com/books

For the full list & description of AnswerGirls titles,
visit the AnswerGirls website:
www.AnswerGirls.com

www.ingramcontent.com/pod-product-compliance
Lightning Source LLC
Chambersburg PA
CBHW071512040426
42444CB00008B/1609